One Launch
METHOD

End The Online Entrepreneur Hustle
And Meet Your Income Goals With...

One Launch

METHOD

LESLIE KLATT

Marketing And Project Management Professional

First edition 2021

Book and cover design by Rens Kivits

ISBN 978-163901586-3

Also By Leslie Klatt:

Lavish Life Planner

Work with Leslie Klatt:

Marketing and Project Management
Online Business Consulting

For Xander and Emerae

Contents

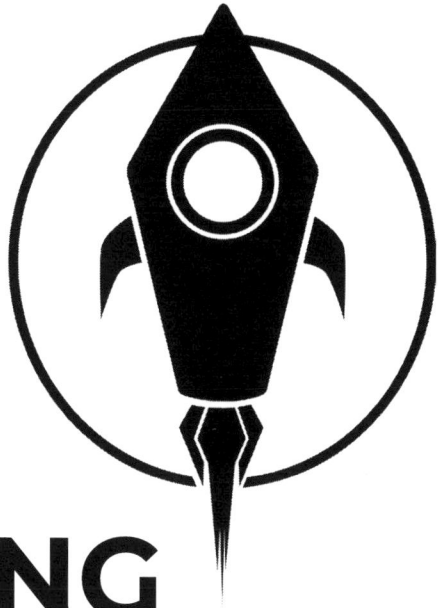

WARNING

Yes, my book comes with a warning.

Everything I'm sharing here is from my education, my experience, my knowledge and real life clients.

I'll be saving you from working in the corporate world, with so many meetings about meetings about meetings.

I'll be saving you from a lot of fluff, a lot of BS, and a lot of false pretences that you need to lose your mind and sacrifice your sanity to be successful.

So here are the warnings:

1. I come up with all my own analogies. At first glance they might seem ridiculous, but they are all relevant.

2. I'm a mom. Many curse words are replaced with things like "banana sandwiches" or "fiddlesticks", but the majority of them are not.

I could blame it on my years working as a project manager in male-dominated industries, where you had to use some shocking language to get the attention on your words instead of dat ass, but I'm not going to, I'll own it.

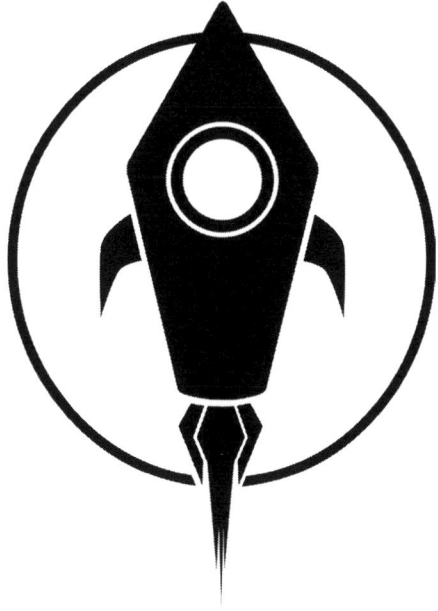

HOW DID WE GET HERE?

It wasn't a big revelation for me. It was a piece by piece process of learning, growing, healing, discovery and realization. It has definitely been a journey, even though that word can be so overused.

What I'm going to share with you in this book is my journey, my knowledge and my experience from studying Marketing in college and working with businesses in corporate environments, starting up my own businesses, building them, selling them and working as a project manager on projects from start-up to multiple billions of dollars.

It wasn't even that long ago that I decided to write this book. I have been running an online business for the last five years. I had invested tens of thousands of dollars in mentors, coaches, courses, books...you name it. And then I stopped.

Why, you ask? Because people have made marketing your business online so weird.

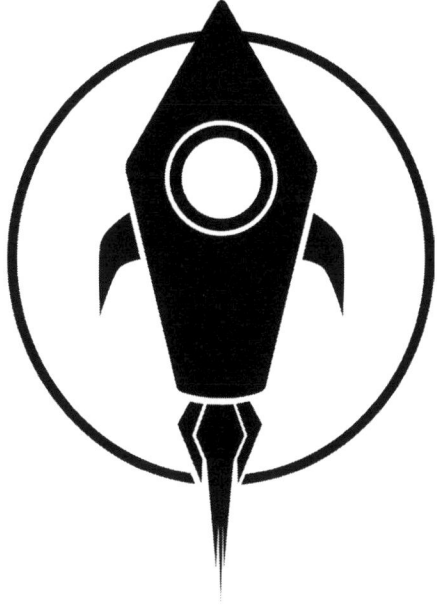

WHO SAYS THAT? I DO

You see, in 2005, after completing my Marketing Diploma in college, followed up by a BA in Political Science and Minor History, I dove right in to Marketing and Business Development.

More specifically, I was setting up businesses online, for myself and as a career.

I had done a little stint in the sales and customer service industry in my hometown, then I scored a major upgrade as a Marketing

Development Manager in the Big City (Greater Toronto Area).

At the same time, since I had my Project Management Professional credential, I was running projects to take this particular company from a local shop and warehouse to a national franchise.

There was website design, contract negotiation, funnel design, which back in the day we just called effective marketing, but now it's a trendy catchy craze – branding, event planning, audience building and grand openings across the country.

Months of preparation, but so worth it, because each location's grand opening had us set up for success from the get go. Clients lined up at the door with credit cards in hand, just waiting for us to say "We're open for business, come on in!"

... One launch, you might say.

What would any entrepreneur-born person do after experiencing that with such success? Open her own business of course.

I designed and created products, negotiated

international manufacturing contracts, created non-competition contracts for the launch of my products and storefronts and imported and distributed well established brands from Ireland, France and Argentina.

I did this in my spare time, after work and on weekends. When the products really started taking off, I sold the contracts to my competitors and would move on to the next project, which was a larger scale product line with higher price tags, and less actual 'work'. We were internationally recognized, featured at top rated events, products were sought after by international conglomerates and it started to get really busy. I sold it, too.

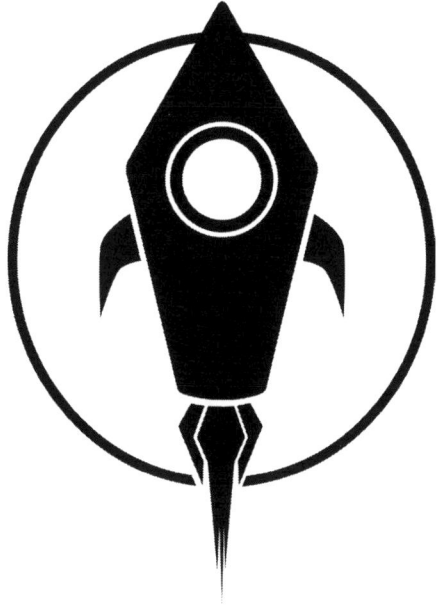

BACK STORY

At this time, when I'm writing this book, I have two kids. They are six and four years old – one boy and one girl.

At this time, when I'm writing this book, I'm a single mom. At this time, when I'm writing this book, I just rebuilt my life after leaving a marriage where I lost absolutely everything, including my home, my horses, my clothes, my dishes and what I thought was my lifelong dream.

I had been working online, a side gig kind of approach, for the last three years, after leaving my full time work on projects, and saw how so many online entrepreneurs are telling people that they need one system, one healing session, or one thing or another to make their business successful.

Since I was the sole provider for my kids now, with almost a million dollars in debt, and having dabbled in all of these 'miracle' type solutions, and not achieving 'miracle' type results from any of them...you know, the webinars, the free five day challenge models, the follow steps 1, 2, 3, so you can achieve A, B, C...those kind of business 'solutions', I kind of just stopped. I had clients and I was getting new clients through referrals and connections on social media.

Now you might be thinking, it must be a mindset thing, right? And after over ten years working in corporate business and project management positions, running my own businesses, it wasn't until I started running business online that I realized just how much inner work and mindset was involved in running businesses.

However...that didn't do it for me either. Well, wait...it did, but it didn't last. Stay tuned – I'll tell you why.

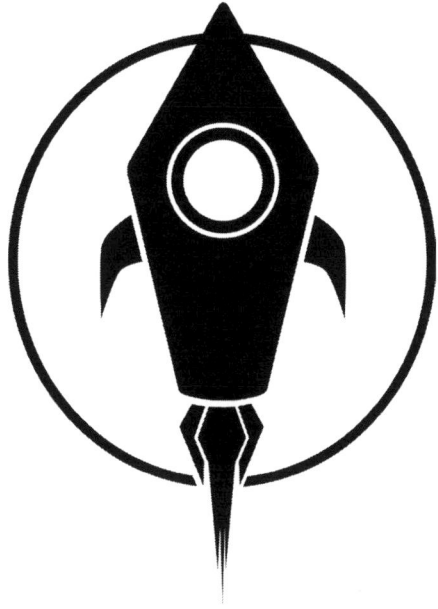

ONLY
QUITTERS
QUIT

I'm not a quitter. At this point, nothing felt 'right'.

There has been this business craze in the last couple of years of running free challenges to build and convert your audience. I'm sure, if you're in the online industry, you've seen a million ads for five day challenges that will change your life. The unfortunate part is that it's pretty rare that they actually do.

But Leslie – how, then, can we give value?

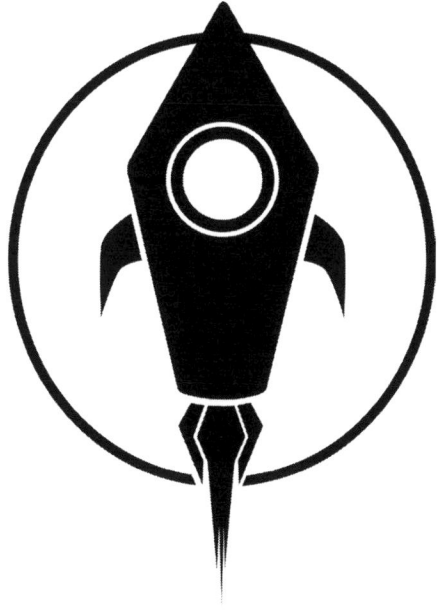

GIVE
GIVE
GIVE
VALUE
VALUE
VALUE

I am so sick of hearing those words. Where do you draw the line?

I'm sure you have an answer for that question. I'm sure an online business coach has given you an answer for that question. And I'm going to tell you it's bullshit.

When you give away the whole cake at the sample table, people are not going to be pleased when they pay you and go home carrying a one ounce paper cup with a spoon scoop of mess in it.

This is exactly what I have seen going on in the online industry. People are giving away their knowledge, their experience and all of the goods. Trusting, ambitious entrepreneurs then invest in their program, service or product and feel cheated because everything was already given to them for free and there is no value on the other side of investing.

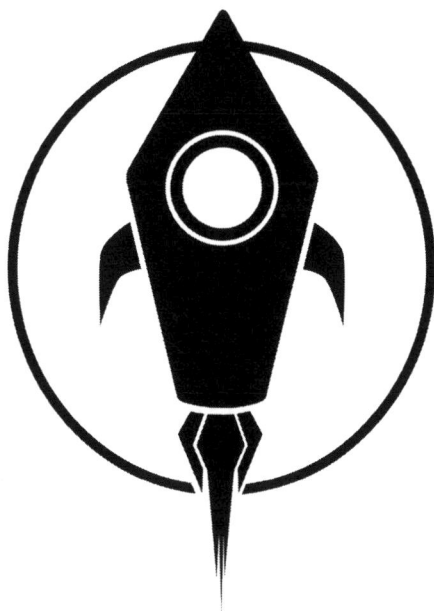

DON'T WORK FOR PEOPLE WHO HAVEN'T HIRED YOU

If you're triggered, you're guilty.

If you have hosted a webinar, a free challenge or even hopped on a consultation or discovery call with potential clients and they say thank you, but they have everything they need to move forward, you are not using these strategies correctly. This is where your marketing message and free sessions need some tweaking.

Chances are, you have heard of the Know, Like And Trust factor. If not, that is perfectly fine. It usually is something that slides off the tip of the tongue of business mentors, but no real explanation is given. That's not my style, so I'm going to show you a method that you can use immediately, to build interest and desire in your products, services and programs, you name it.

I've dubbed it the 'KLT Method'. It is a method of copy writing and speaking that allows your potential clients to Know what you do and who you serve, Like your methods and connect with you and Trust that you will deliver exactly what they need.

You do this by helping your potential clients identify what the issue actually is. Many people will seek help from one source or another and are left feeling cheated because their desired result was not achieved.

The problem here is not necessarily that the service was not provided, but that the client bought into something that didn't actually solve what their problem really was.

If your dog pulls on the leash like a crazy beast every time you walk her – this might be a real story – the issue isn't that you need to wear gloves when you go for walks and work out more to build upper body strength. But if you want that dog to stop pulling you need to work on getting the dog's attention on you, help her confidence issues, build a tighter bond, things that are beyond the surface.

The same can be said for the issues that your clients want or need to correct in their life or business. It might seem like they need a new website, or someone to write their email sequences for them, so they hire someone to do that and still end up with the same underlying issue at hand.

So you, the expert, have to know what the long term effects are of not correcting the issues that you resolve for your clients and you need to make them aware of that. This is how they get to KNOW what you do. This is real value that is marketing your business and not just giving it all away.

And, if you want your potential clients to know about your products and services, you have to know what they are first. This is where entrepreneurship can get really deep and self discovery happens so that your own belief in your product or service is so strong that you are unshakeable. So that your message is so clear that there is no question about what you do and for whom.

This is how you will build life long, raving fans.

I worked with a client once who was already making multiple seven figures when we were getting her podcast launch together. To most, making seven figures is an amazing and admirable feat.

We set up her plan, she loved it. She shared it with her mastermind community and had full support from everyone in her network. This was going to be amazing!

Her team started working on the launch plan and kept making suggestions that they saw other people doing in their businesses that they claimed brought them big success.

The funny thing is, they had about six different ways that other entrepreneurs had set up their podcasts, and everyone started getting a serious feeling of comparisonitis.

"If we aren't doing things the way these successful people have done it, we must be doing it wrong then."

"I don't want to screw it up".

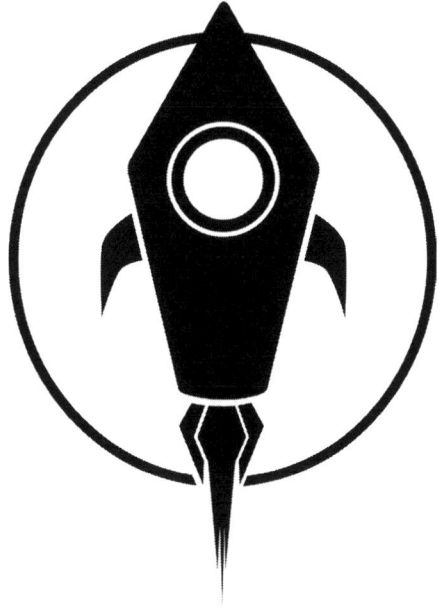

YOU ARE BEING YOURSELF YOU CANNOT SCREW IT UP

None of my clients' businesses look identical. Yes, they all use the principles of the One Launch Method. That's as far as the similarities go.

I even go further to make sure that they aren't suggesting that they want to mimic a concept that they've seen another client use, because of the successes they've experienced, with our one on one coaching time and get to the real answer of what works for them and what does not.

That accounts for everything from their copy schedule, their publications, topics, product or service hosting, delivery systems and branding, all of it. So when there is a plan in place it is a plan that will give you and your clients optimal results.

So if you tell me that you want to copy a template or a 'funnel' that brought someone else success because you're afraid that yours is not the same as theirs, you might want to then try to download all of their knowledge and experience into your mind, change your offer to be what theirs is, connect with their audience, change your life around to match their schedule, their goals, their lifestyle, and all of their things, because it is *their marketing message and their marketing plan.*

If you would like to sell out your own product or service, let's set you up with your very own message and plan, instead of creating the failure that you are trying to avoid.

My client Lynn, the Maritime Mystic, has incredible talent, education, experience and a real story to share and inspire, to help people reconnect with their intuition, develop trust in themselves to change their lives and truly experience grounding, decision making and fulfillment. She is an Acupuncturist, a sought out Reader and an Artist who is setting up for a big launch this year with her first online program.

Now, everybody knows that in order to make sales online, you need the leads. And often what happens is you set out to see how other people got those leads.

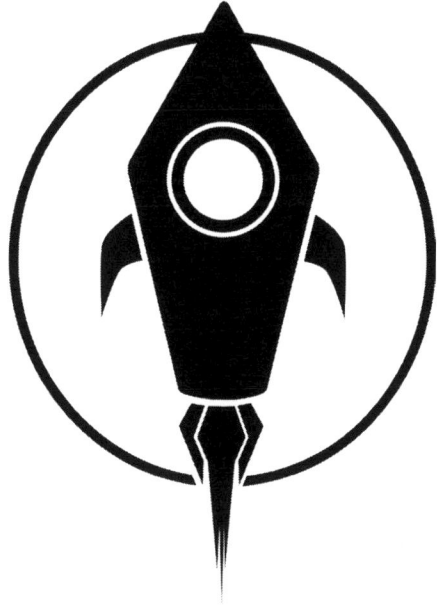

IT'S MARKETING, NOT A POPULARITY CONTEST

Things I hear: "Look at this YouTube channel. This one girl has hundreds of thousands of subscribers, so clearly, for me to reach that kind of success, I have to do what she did."

My lovely Lynn had a list of videos, as a guideline, that she wanted to create to build her audience. She shared the list with me and what we noticed after asking some questions was that she wouldn't necessarily be attracting her ideal clients. She could get some big numbers, but I'm always after quality, not quantity. Some focus on her expertise, knowledge, experience had to happen.

Be confident in what you offer and let people know what that is without wavering.

Questions to ask yourself, when you find your marketing plan is made up of a frankenbusiness mess of other entrepreneurs' strategies.

What are they selling?
What am I selling?

Who is their audience?
Who is my audience?

How are they hosting their clients?
How am I hosting my clients?

What is their knowledge and experience?
What is my knowledge and experience?

This looks a lot like comparison, and it is. It's competitive analysis and what you will find at the end is that there is no comparison. This is how you will find your unique positioning that you are going to lean into big time to attract YOUR ideal clients, build YOUR leads and create YOUR very own marketing plan.

So Lynn set up her plan to let the world know how her clients overcome their fears, doubts and 'stuck' points with her program and she set up her One Launch effortlessly, just by defining and deciding her 'know' factor.

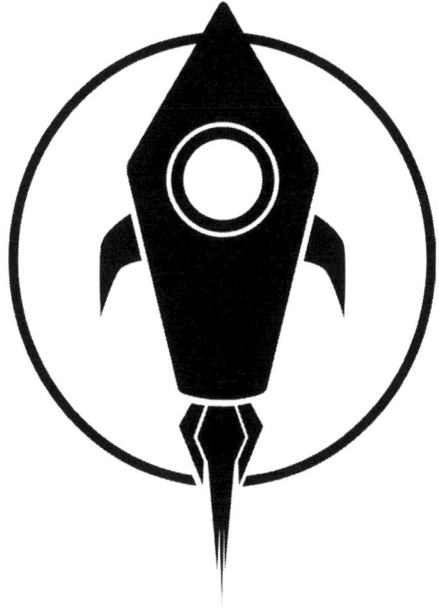

YOU GET TO DECIDE

You get to decide and you have to decide. What part of that made you cringe? Once you've done that competitive analysis and you know exactly how you stand out and what your Know, Like and Trust Factors will be, you get to stop making decisions and you get to start building your launch, your One Launch.

We can all be inspired and have some interest in many different things, I get it. Many of us all wear a 'multi passionista' badge, but when it comes to your business, you have to decide on what your focus will be.

If everything gets a little bit of your focus, none of these things will grow to their full potential. This is not the kind of result that my clients are after. With One Launch Method, we focus on your big ticket, claim to fame offer, and we make it big!

Things I hear: "I've done this before and it worked though. So I should do it again." or "Well my current audience is really into xyz."

These things do not matter. What matters is what you want for your business, what your dream program, product or service is and that is what we are going to make you famous for! World renowned kind of recognition.

My client Rhian, who is a Sex and Relationship Therapist, has developed an amazing program to help people who have experienced trauma from a past relationship that holds them back from trusting, loving and even living their lives. Post Traumatic Relationship Syndrome. She has been recognized for her work in the spiritual industry for many years and was holding on to that as it is what her current audience and old fans had known her for.

As she developed her PTRS content and One Launch plan for her legacy program to help and heal people who are suffering from relationship trauma, the rest felt out of place.

She decided it was time to focus. PTRS was her dream program and even talking about it lit her up. As she focused on her One Launch program, all of the pieces started falling into place. Her energy toward the business shifted, opportunities arose and her One Launch is set up and already being recognized as the Holy Grail that the relationship therapy and coaching industry has been searching for.

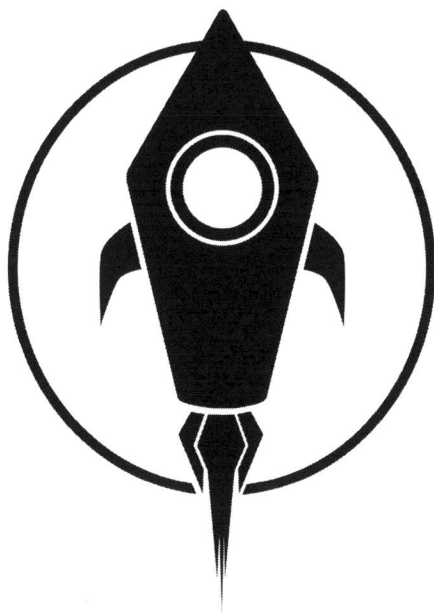

THIS IS YOUR WORLD NOW

This is where things shift from hustle to impact. This is what I love the most! You get to stop trying.

I have seen so many entrepreneurs come out with a new product, program or service and start introducing their methods on social media. Perfect! You will find ideal clients on social media, but you will not find them by introducing your signature product, program, or service in the form of a question. Some see this as a form of market research, but it is not setting you up as an unshakeable CEO.

Asking for favours in your meek little posts does not a successful business make.

You have decided what your offer is. This is all you are showing people now. It is not time to ask questions, it's time to schedule your parade and start the party!

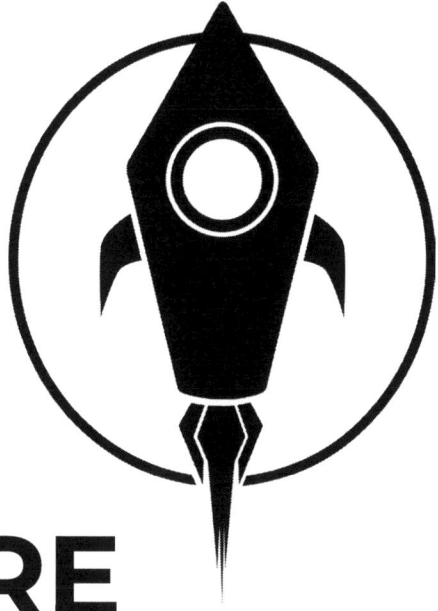

FANFARE BABY

Everybody knows what's coming, when you have that focus, when you are unshakeable in your vision. It's not going to be a big surprise, but your audience will be on the edge of their seats when the time comes.

When you line up for the Santa Claus parade you know at the end of this parade, there is going to be a big guy in a suit with some reindeer and a big white beard. People aren't just going to show up for Santa's float though, they are here for the whole show.

Give the people what they want. They want a

whole show. Everything in the parade has to do with Christmas. It's my favourite holiday.

You know the Santa Claus float (your offer) is gold. That's what people are waiting for. They're excited the entire time, but Santa is the main event of the parade!

This is the kind of excitement and fanfare that you have to build for your offer. They've seen where you've been featured in articles, they've seen your videos, they've heard your theories, concepts, and benefits of your product, program, or service. You have been focused and nobody is confused about your knowledge, experience or education on the matter.

The marching band is going full force!
They're dancing in the streets!
Gasp! It's launch day!
Gasp! I hear the jingle bells!

That is the kind of fanfare that we're looking for. You don't have to be sneaky about what you're doing. You don't have to be sneaky about what your offer is. You don't have to be sneaky about the fact that you're going to sell something. You just get to be excited about it and build the excitement with your audience.

It's not about tricking people into buying something, it's about creating desire and excitement for what you're offering. Creating that 'save-the-date', 'mark it in your calendars because my launch is coming' kind of excitement, and rolling out the red carpet for it.

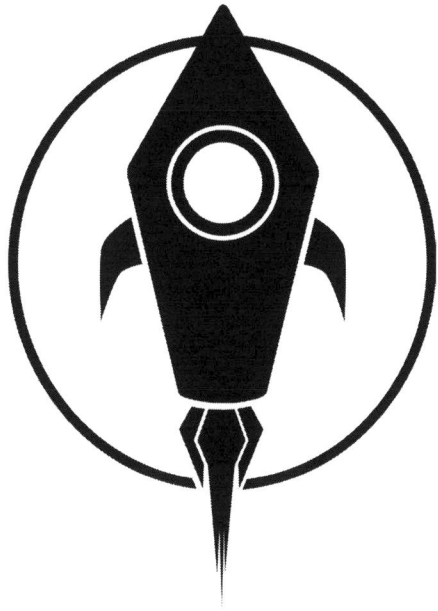

BUT I'M NOT SANTA CLAUS

That's okay dear. We're gonna make you into Santa Claus! This is your placement. Where should you be? Who should you be mingling with?

The best part and the most difficult part of placement is that it's not a 'you have to sit at the kids' table until you're 14' kind of a situation. This is another thing you get to decide and just go for it.

You want to be where your people are.

A little ode to my favourite childhood movie. Your fanfare, your lead up to the launch, your positioning, your reputation...these are the things that we're going to cover and these are the things that are so detrimental to the success of your launch when you haven't got them right.

You really have to know who you want to be working with, where they are and where you want to be. That is where you will set yourself up.

In the One Launch Method this is where we set up your framework. We set up your big vision, not as a start up, not as a 'let's just get your first client' kind of approach. If you're doing One Launch to make your income for the year, it has to support the life you want to live. So we set up the framework to achieve your goals.

If you have decided that you are a luxury brand that you are selling high-ticket packages to high-performing people, you will not be selling five dollar DIY services and hustlin' to make a hundred sales a month, or a thousand, or wherever your goal may be.

We will be positioning you where you want to be in the market and that is exactly where you belong. You have to know what you want, you have to know who you're going to work with and you have to position yourself there and commit to it.

My client Corina – Auntie Corina – is a Parenting Support Coach for Entrepreneurs. She has decades of experience and education in raising her own children, running an inhome daycare as well as formal education in behaviour, psychology and child education. She has simplified her methods into three pillars that can solve any parenting problem, which is so crucial when you work from home and which she has heard from every podcaster, publication, blog and summit she has been invited to and been featured on.

There were no janky posts on social media. There were no meek and mild marketing tactics. There was knowing where she wanted to be and being there.

She is now launching her Positive Parenting For Entrepreneurs program for high-level and high-performing entrepreneurs with international recognition. That's how you set yourself up!

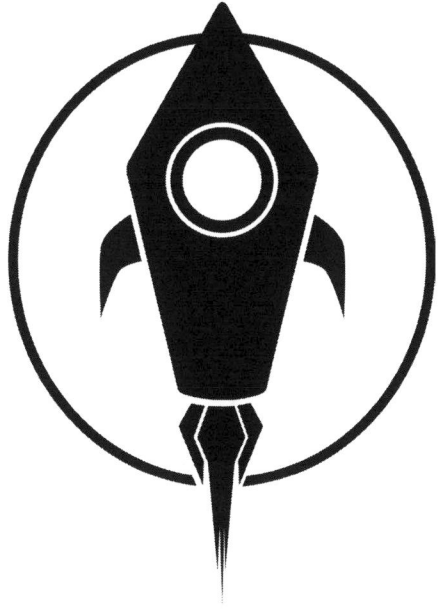

MAKE SPACE FOR WHAT YOU WANT

Visualize it and make it real. Dream big and have a tangible goal.

I think it's safe to say in order to be inspired to start something like a business, there was a vision. Yes?

What you get to do now is live that. This is why, in the One Launch Method, we set up the framework to support your goal. This is why we position you where you want to be.

You get to make space for exactly what you want in your life. The clients, the events, the sales, the opportunities and the lifestyle. So let's write it down so that it isn't just an idea in your head that will pass and then come back to haunt you or remind you that you haven't actually done anything to make it real yet.

Some will visualize all of this luxury and say things like "I want to make as much money as possible and work with as many clients as possible." I had a client that did this, and I just told him "No. As much as possible is not something you can ever achieve!"

Triggered? Good. That means that a change is afoot, where you can stop hustling and feeling like nothing that you do is ever enough or that you could have done more, and you can see your efforts start to pay off. This is where it stops being a hustle, a grind, a lose your mind hobby that you call a business and you get to be an unshakeable CEO with measurable action steps to take toward your measurable goals.

This is how you get to have a successful business and know when and how to scale it. And I'm going to get really real with you and I want you to get real with yourself too. I am all about dreaming, I'm all about doodling plans and making them come true.

When I was seven years old I was given a book. My neighbour was a Bank Manager, and they were transitioning from paper ledger books to computers. When she gave me this book, my sister and I doodled on the cover of it. She showed me how to draw this cute cartoon cat – she is 100% a better artist than I am.

But what I did was let my most remarkable dreaming skills and natural talent for visualization take over and I drew a house.

This wasn't just a box with windows and an 'm' shaped seagull flying overhead. Every single brick was drawn, the shingles for the roof, the driveway and the flowers that lined the driveway.

It gets even better and you're going to be reading this and thinking "Wow Leslie, now I see why you ended up being a Project Manager." Or you might just think I'm crazy.

I drew every room in the house. The floor plan, yes, but I also set up every single room, one page per room, the pillows, the towels in the bathroom, the hangers in the closet, the names for the horses, the cow, just one cow, the bunnies, the big dogs and the little dogs. Every detail was there.

That's the kind of visualization I'm talking

about here, for you. Every aspect of your life including your business.

> *What do you want?*
> *How do you want it to feel?*
> *What do you need to make it happen?*

You can experience this all right now. There is no 'baby business'. Just make the space for it to happen. I really want you to see how this can happen, because when I started living life this way, it changed so much. Part of the problem that I have witnessed in the last five years, working strictly online with entrepreneurs, is that they're set up to run their business one way, but what they actually want to achieve is something completely different.

If you have plugged your dream, your visualization into a form, a mold, or something that you don't actually want, at all, at what point, do you decide to stop that and completely restructure?

I have had many conversations with entrepreneurs who come to me when they are sick of dedicating their lives to a beast of a business that they grew themselves and they're burnt out. They have started to hate their business and resent their clients and they just cannot do it anymore.

And here's the story I've heard many times – they've been running their business online, they have clients, they have seen success, and those successes can range anywhere from a couple of thousand dollars a month to tens of thousands per month.

The struggles are the same, at the edge of every stage, but lucky for us, so is the solution.

So, they take a month off or sometimes two and they come back with a new launch, and do it all over again. They hustle, they launch, they make money, they show up for a bit, they burn out, they leave, they come back.

One of the first things I want us to know is how you want your business to fit in with your life. What is your goal? Visualize and dream, write it down, set up the framework and start experiencing those things at whatever level as soon as today.

How many hours do you work? What do you

do in the evenings? What do you do on the weekends? Think of everything and follow that ideal model.

This whole hustle model that people have been idolizing is pure exhaustion. People bragging that they're busier than the other, or have more irons in the fire. This is not ideal to me.

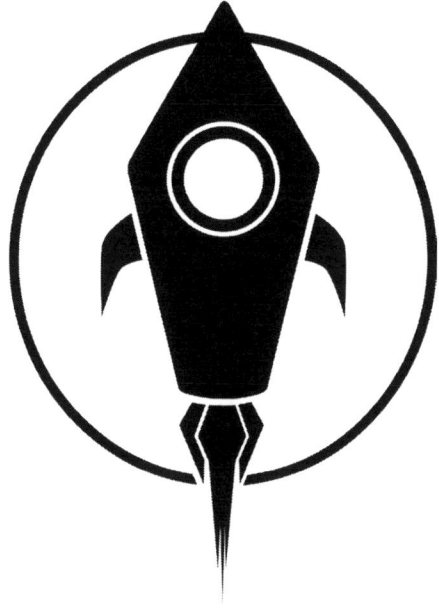

NO MORE HUSTLE

My first recommendation would be to stop. Allow yourself to feel some form of relaxation.

Then allow yourself to embrace your positioning, make a serious and solid impact in your online marketing efforts and you will automatically start showing up stronger and you will effortlessly start to attract the people who are going to be your biggest fans.

Otherwise, you will be constantly chasing your tail or trying to come up with ideas, like throwing spaghetti at the wall, to get more likes with funny cat memes and weird engagementment posts that don't help conversion rates and leave you with an insane and completely unsustainable level of hustle and content creation, Gary Vee style.

Obviously, Gary is successful, but for you to achieve the amount of content he shares every day, and be everywhere like he is, is going to lead you to exhaustion. He has an entire team that works for him, documenting his every word and then they create that content for him. I'm not saying that what you've been doing in your business is wrong, I'm just saying that there is a better way.

You can effectively market and launch your product, program, or service without having your nose in your phone constantly or have a team of people working for you to document your every move.

When you move forward with a clear focus and your end goal framework in place with systems to support it, you do not have to hustle, you do not have to go live every single day with a genius piece of advice or just to get attention. You get to build purposeful content that allows your audience to see consistency and build trust.

If your content is all over the place, showcasing several concepts, even if it's just something that interests you, it can cause confusion when you are using social media for marketing. A confused audience will not be ready to purchase.

This is where a lot of entrepreneurs get frustrated when they're showing up constantly, getting a lot of likes on their posts, but nobody is buying their products, programs or services. It's because the content lacks consistency and the Trust factor isn't built yet. Your audience does not yet trust that you will deliver the results you are promising.

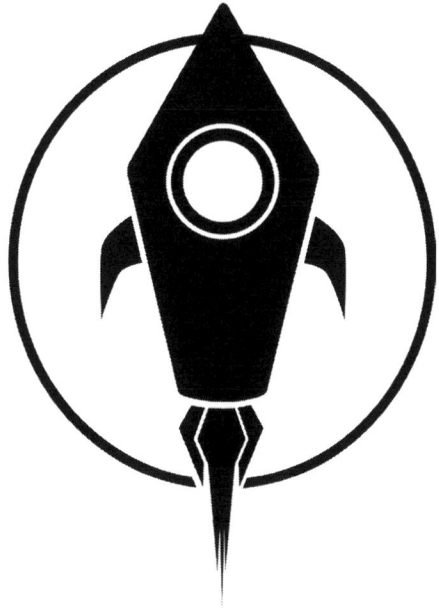

KEEP
IT SIMPLE

Let's make it a clean cut and simple way to set up your business. Some popular tactics that people have been convinced to follow in the last few years have appeared so weird to me.

When you set up a business plan – a real, take it to the bank kind of business plan, there are no five day challenges, there are no camera crews and no content creation. It's about forecasting.

Keep it simple, hustle-free and to the point, with consistent marketing and growth so that you have measurable statistics and can actually see what works and what doesn't. This is how my clients are able to develop an idea, get clear on it, focus their message and marketing efforts and have One Launch to make their yearly income in under three months.

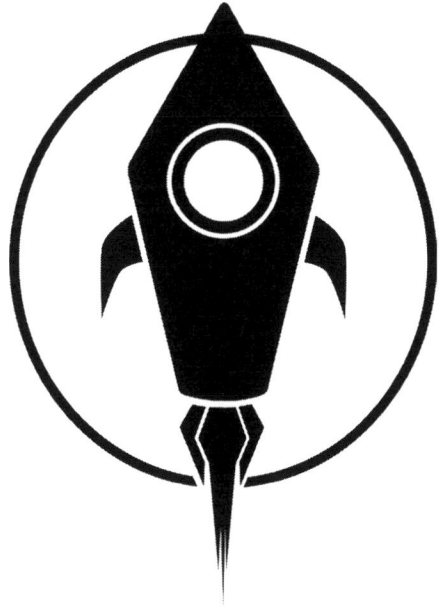

BUILD YOUR RIVER BANKS

The words 'plan' and 'flow' with business and inspired action are often used opposingly, like one way is more ideal than the other. Here is what I think.

You need a plan to be able to flow. It's like a river bank. Picture this – you're dropped off by a helicopter, with a floaty and no oars.

Question – will you get from point A to point B faster if you're dropped off in an ocean or a river? Answer – river! Because the river has banks. It has a framework, it has structure and it leads directly to point B.

Let's get your vision set up into a plan so that your One Launch can be successful! If you're ready to stop hustling and you want to set up your business to reflect what you actually desire, run through this exercise and get your plan together. This is the most effective way to take serious impactful action in your business, you will show yourself and your team – your employees, investors and partners – that you are committed to building the business that you have been dreaming of.

I like to do this for one and three year growth plans.

1. Set up and celebrate milestones. Your plan is going to highlight your vision and set up long-term milestones that are most important to the success of your business.

2. Understand your company's advantages. Get real and get deep with your 'stand out' marketability. When you document the how, when and why your business will grow and every reason why your clients will invest with

you is crystal clear.

3. Understand your customer. Why do they buy when they buy? Why don't they when they don't? Look into the psychology and behaviour of your ideal customer to place your launch and growth strategies.

4. Avoid assumptions. If you have found yourself focused on something that has held your business stagnant or have completely overlooked something critical to your business success, seeing everything written down will allow you to see any missed steps.

5. Document your revenue model. Decide how much cash your One Launch is going to bring you and then we can set up your plan to make it happen!

6. Pursue all the right opportunities. When you have your plan set up you can easily reach out for opportunities and decline those that will not move your business ahead.

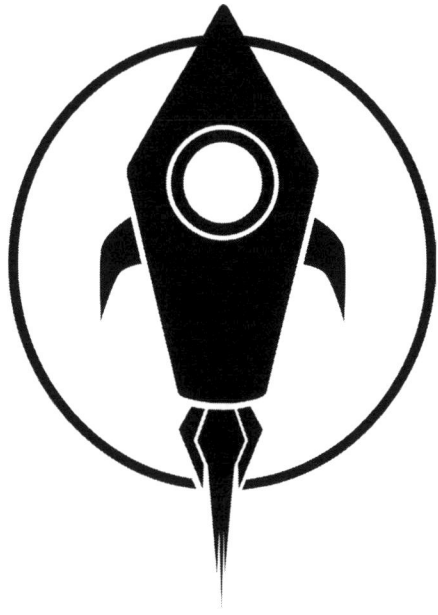

STICK
TO
THE PLAN

When you have your plan in place and know where you want to go, how you want to get there and when, we can use the One Launch Method framework to fill it all in and make it happen.

Your messaging will attract your ideal clients and build trust in record time because your focus will be unshakeable and your positioning will be second to none. And as you work through each step and gain your recognition you will be showing up to your own parade with such confidence that your raving fans will be there, waiting for the opportunity to invest in your offer!

Now make sure you follow through on your end of the deal. How are you hosting your clients? Having systems in place to do this will give your clients the best experience with you, as human error can be removed from the equation.

There are no excuses now like "Oh, I was having a bad day." Or maybe your kids are going crazy when someone is attempting to purchase your product, program or service. I'm not going to tell you what this looks like either. When I work with my clients through the One Launch Method, the client experience is, once again, unique.

What works for you?

What information do your clients need to receive right away, since they should receive something immediately?

What is their next step?

Be a good hostess, allow your clients'

experience to be another boost of confidence for them, so that they know they made the right choice by investing with you.

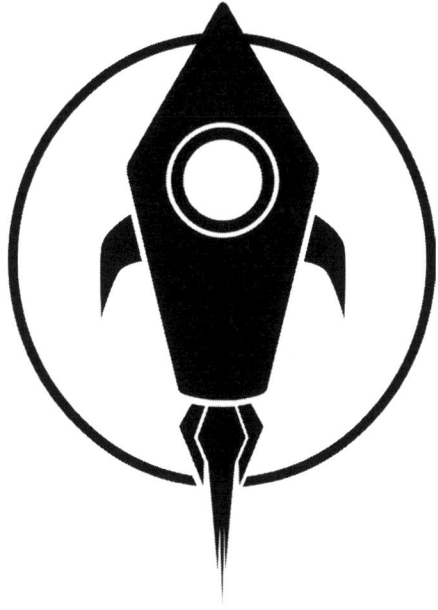

GET OUT OF THE WAY

How to make it impossible to fail? Believe in what you're offering 100%.

The One Launch Method might not be for you if you love giving in to your fear and doubts. This system is set up to make those fears and doubts take a back seat while you prove to yourself that you don't have to hold on to them anymore. Pull over and let them out at the next intersection.

This is not about putting your ideal life on a pedestal and saying "Will that be me one day?"

I have news for you, today is a day and this is you. What are you doing about it?

If you look at your life and business right now and it is not what you want it to be, it's not set up the way you think it should be when you're making millions of dollars a year, why isn't it? How can it be? When do you get to stop setting yourself up to be small?

When you follow the One Launch Method, the framework and the schedule, the fanfare and the goals will pull you away from that fear, because it is going to happen.

When I was in high school, I was on the rowing team. I was in the 'stroke' position in an 'eight'. That info is just for visual effect. The coxswain would be yelling in my face as I rowed and the crew followed my stroke.

Every person in that boat was critical. If someone didn't show up for 5am practice or a regatta, we would literally be going in circles. We actually just wouldn't row. So let's say everybody showed up and we were on the water. Eight oars in the water, eight rowers at the ready, scrunched up with arms extended to drop the oar in the water, to get this boat up and moving.

In this story I want you to think of you as each rower and a part of your One Launch as an oar and stick with me here.

The cox yells out for you to start rowing and you pull two of the oars out of the water, drop two in right off the rigging and into the water, only give half stroke on a couple of them and give it everything you've got on the last two.

That boat is not going anywhere. It might even flip. You're going to be in the lake with snapping turtles and seaweed wondering why your launch wasn't a great success.

Yes, snapping turtles were an issue in the lake we rowed on every morning at 5am for three years of my life. And I don't want you to get snapped.

There is this amazing feeling, just thinking about it actually made me sigh with joy, when you keep your eyes up, your movement in sync, and there is equal amount of power given to every single oar. The boat lifts out of the water. It skims the surface, it glides across the lake, and the motion of the boat, of the oars – plunk, plunk, plunk – it keeps you in check too.

The slide up, the plunk of the oar, the pull and push of your body...the kilometers of the race just sail past and you make it to the finish line feeling like you just had a spiritual awakening, because you have, and every oar, every task you had to complete, every article you wrote, every podcast you were featured on, every graphic, email and video you created made it to your destination.

The One Launch that has brought you more recognition, more raving fans, more clients and income than any hustle, struggle, dropping the ball and beating yourself up, to only 'try' again ever could have.

It's not about fixing your fear before you do the thing. You have to do the thing in spite of the fear or you will end up making the very thing that you're scared of become your reality.

Don't pull your oars out and flip your boat trying to avoid the snapping turtles. That's exactly why you have to keep your oars in and give it all you've got. That's the one way you can guarantee you won't get snapped.

If you were wondering how One Launch Method works, that's it.

A letter from leslie

Thank you so much for reading through the One Launch Method. I hope that the stories and concepts will help you with your vision and your goals in your life and business.

I am always available to help you get your business started or to get you set up and launching to the next level.

The One Launch Method, as a program, is a three month process. Yes, that's it. You can set your vision up and market it effectively to have your results in the bank in three months, tops.

I invite you to access my members' area where you can work through your business plan right away and see where you need to beef things up.

If I can be of any assistance, just reach out and book a time for a call to go over your vision, your plans, and your One Launch to end the online entrepreneurial hustle!

I can't wait to hear your plans!

Chat soon,
Leslie

Your One Launch

Let's not over complicate things now. When you have decided that you are ready to launch your next big thing, put all of the principles in this book to work right away.

You can go from idea to successful launch in under three months.

When I work with my clients we have planning and online software that we work with, but I've included a basic launch tracker and daily action sheets for you here.

Write down your vision and goals, track your networking and leads, take focused action steps every day and you can experience true entrepreneurial freedom.

ONE LAUNCH

TRACKING

OFFER

LAUNH DATE: ....

PRICE: ....

AUDIENCE: ....

....

....

SOCIAL PLATFORMS: ....

....

....

....

PUBLICATIONS: ....

....

....

....

....

COLLABORATIONS: ....

....

....

....

LANDING PAGE DOMAIN: ....

....

....

....

- [ ] FREE OFFER
- [ ] EMAIL SEQUENCES
- [ ] PROMO CONTENT
- [ ] LAUNCH EVENT
- [ ] ....
- [ ] ....
- [ ] ....
- [ ] ....
- [ ] ....
- [ ] ....
- [ ] ....
- [ ] ....
- [ ] ....

DAILY ACTION SHEETS

ONE LAUNCH METHOD

DATE TODAY: _____

MOVE YOUR BUSINESS FORWARD:

- [ ] _____
- [ ] _____
- [ ] _____
- [ ] _____
- [ ] _____
- [ ] _____
- [ ] _____
- [ ] _____

APPOINTMENTS:

NEW CONTACTS AND FOLLOW UP:

DAILY ACTION SHEETS

ONE LAUNCH METHOD

DATE TODAY: ─────────────

MOVE YOUR BUSINESS FORWARD: APPOINTMENTS:

☐ _____

☐ _____

☐ _____

☐ _____

☐ _____

☐ _____

☐ _____

☐ _____

NEW CONTACTS AND FOLLOW UP:

DAILY ACTION SHEETS

ONE LAUNCH METHOD

DATE TODAY: ━━━━━━━━━━

MOVE YOUR BUSINESS FORWARD:

☐ _____

☐ _____

☐ _____

☐ _____

☐ _____

☐ _____

☐ _____

☐ _____

APPOINTMENTS:

NEW CONTACTS AND FOLLOW UP:

DAILY ACTION SHEETS

ONE LAUNCH METHOD

DATE TODAY: ─────────────────

MOVE YOUR BUSINESS FORWARD: APPOINTMENTS:

☐ _____

☐ _____

☐ _____

☐ _____

☐ _____

☐ _____

☐ _____

☐ _____

NEW CONTACTS AND FOLLOW UP:

DAILY ACTION SHEETS

ONE LAUNCH METHOD

DATE TODAY: ━━━━━━━━━━━━━

MOVE YOUR BUSINESS FORWARD:

APPOINTMENTS:

☐ _____

☐ _____

☐ _____

☐ _____

☐ _____

☐ _____

☐ _____

☐ _____

NEW CONTACTS AND FOLLOW UP:

DAILY ACTION SHEETS

ONE LAUNCH METHOD

DATE TODAY: —————————

MOVE YOUR BUSINESS FORWARD:

APPOINTMENTS:

- [ ] _____
- [ ] _____
- [ ] _____
- [ ] _____
- [ ] _____
- [ ] _____
- [ ] _____
- [ ] _____

NEW CONTACTS AND FOLLOW UP:

DAILY ACTION SHEETS

ONE LAUNCH METHOD

DATE TODAY: ─────────────

MOVE YOUR BUSINESS FORWARD: APPOINTMENTS:

☐ _____

☐ _____

☐ _____

☐ _____

☐ _____

☐ _____

☐ _____

☐ _____

NEW CONTACTS AND FOLLOW UP:

DAILY ACTION SHEETS

ONE LAUNCH METHOD

DATE TODAY: _____

MOVE YOUR BUSINESS FORWARD:

APPOINTMENTS:

- [ ] _____
- [ ] _____
- [ ] _____
- [ ] _____
- [ ] _____
- [ ] _____
- [ ] _____
- [ ] _____

NEW CONTACTS AND FOLLOW UP:

DAILY ACTION SHEETS

ONE LAUNCH METHOD

DATE TODAY: ─────────────

MOVE YOUR BUSINESS FORWARD:

APPOINTMENTS:

☐ _____

☐ _____

☐ _____

☐ _____

☐ _____

☐ _____

☐ _____

☐ _____

NEW CONTACTS AND FOLLOW UP:

DAILY ACTION SHEETS

ONE LAUNCH METHOD

DATE TODAY: ————————

MOVE YOUR BUSINESS FORWARD:

APPOINTMENTS:

- [ ] _____
- [ ] _____
- [ ] _____
- [ ] _____
- [ ] _____
- [ ] _____
- [ ] _____
- [ ] _____

NEW CONTACTS AND FOLLOW UP:

DAILY ACTION SHEETS

ONE LAUNCH METHOD

DATE TODAY: _____

MOVE YOUR BUSINESS FORWARD:

☐ _____

☐ _____

☐ _____

☐ _____

☐ _____

☐ _____

☐ _____

☐ _____

APPOINTMENTS:

NEW CONTACTS AND FOLLOW UP:

DAILY ACTION SHEETS

ONE LAUNCH METHOD

DATE TODAY: ————————————

MOVE YOUR BUSINESS FORWARD:

- [ ] _____
- [ ] _____
- [ ] _____
- [ ] _____
- [ ] _____
- [ ] _____
- [ ] _____
- [ ] _____

APPOINTMENTS:

NEW CONTACTS AND FOLLOW UP:

DAILY ACTION SHEETS

ONE LAUNCH METHOD

DATE TODAY: ━━━━━━━━━━━━

MOVE YOUR BUSINESS FORWARD:

APPOINTMENTS:

- ☐ _____
- ☐ _____
- ☐ _____
- ☐ _____
- ☐ _____
- ☐ _____
- ☐ _____
- ☐ _____

NEW CONTACTS AND FOLLOW UP:

DAILY ACTION SHEETS

ONE LAUNCH METHOD

DATE TODAY: ⎯⎯⎯⎯⎯⎯⎯⎯

MOVE YOUR BUSINESS FORWARD: APPOINTMENTS:

- [ ] _____
- [ ] _____
- [ ] _____
- [ ] _____
- [ ] _____
- [ ] _____
- [ ] _____
- [ ] _____

NEW CONTACTS AND FOLLOW UP:

DAILY ACTION SHEETS

ONE LAUNCH METHOD

DATE TODAY: ————————————

MOVE YOUR BUSINESS FORWARD:

- [ ] _____
- [ ] _____
- [ ] _____
- [ ] _____
- [ ] _____
- [ ] _____
- [ ] _____
- [ ] _____

APPOINTMENTS:

NEW CONTACTS AND FOLLOW UP:

DAILY ACTION SHEETS

ONE LAUNCH METHOD

DATE TODAY: ——————————

MOVE YOUR BUSINESS FORWARD:

- [ ] _____
- [ ] _____
- [ ] _____
- [ ] _____
- [ ] _____
- [ ] _____
- [ ] _____
- [ ] _____

APPOINTMENTS:

NEW CONTACTS AND FOLLOW UP:

DAILY ACTION SHEETS

ONE LAUNCH METHOD

DATE TODAY: ——————————

MOVE YOUR BUSINESS FORWARD:

APPOINTMENTS:

- [ ] _____
- [ ] _____
- [ ] _____
- [ ] _____
- [ ] _____
- [ ] _____
- [ ] _____
- [ ] _____

NEW CONTACTS AND FOLLOW UP:

DAILY ACTION SHEETS

ONE LAUNCH METHOD

DATE TODAY: _____

MOVE YOUR BUSINESS FORWARD: APPOINTMENTS:

☐ _____

☐ _____

☐ _____

☐ _____

☐ _____

☐ _____

☐ _____

☐ _____

NEW CONTACTS AND FOLLOW UP:

DAILY ACTION SHEETS

ONE LAUNCH METHOD

DATE TODAY: _____

MOVE YOUR BUSINESS FORWARD:

☐ _____
☐ _____
☐ _____
☐ _____
☐ _____
☐ _____
☐ _____
☐ _____

APPOINTMENTS:

NEW CONTACTS AND FOLLOW UP:

DAILY ACTION SHEETS

ONE LAUNCH METHOD

DATE TODAY: _____

MOVE YOUR BUSINESS FORWARD:

- ☐ _____
- ☐ _____
- ☐ _____
- ☐ _____
- ☐ _____
- ☐ _____
- ☐ _____
- ☐ _____

APPOINTMENTS:

NEW CONTACTS AND FOLLOW UP:

DAILY ACTION SHEETS

ONE LAUNCH METHOD

DATE TODAY: ━━━━━━━━━━

MOVE YOUR BUSINESS FORWARD:

☐ _____

☐ _____

☐ _____

☐ _____

☐ _____

☐ _____

☐ _____

☐ _____

APPOINTMENTS:

NEW CONTACTS AND FOLLOW UP:

DAILY ACTION SHEETS

ONE LAUNCH METHOD

DATE TODAY: _____

MOVE YOUR BUSINESS FORWARD:

APPOINTMENTS:

- [ ] _____
- [ ] _____
- [ ] _____
- [ ] _____
- [ ] _____
- [ ] _____
- [ ] _____
- [ ] _____

NEW CONTACTS AND FOLLOW UP:

DAILY ACTION SHEETS

ONE LAUNCH METHOD

DATE TODAY: ━━━━━━━━━━

MOVE YOUR BUSINESS FORWARD:

APPOINTMENTS:

- [ ] _____
- [ ] _____
- [ ] _____
- [ ] _____
- [ ] _____
- [ ] _____
- [ ] _____
- [ ] _____

NEW CONTACTS AND FOLLOW UP:

DAILY ACTION SHEETS

ONE LAUNCH METHOD

DATE TODAY: ————————————

MOVE YOUR BUSINESS FORWARD: APPOINTMENTS:

- [ ] _____
- [ ] _____
- [ ] _____
- [ ] _____
- [ ] _____
- [ ] _____
- [ ] _____
- [ ] _____

NEW CONTACTS AND FOLLOW UP:

DAILY ACTION SHEETS

ONE LAUNCH METHOD

DATE TODAY: ⏤⏤⏤⏤⏤

MOVE YOUR BUSINESS FORWARD:

APPOINTMENTS:

☐ _____

☐ _____

☐ _____

☐ _____

☐ _____

☐ _____

☐ _____

☐ _____

NEW CONTACTS AND FOLLOW UP:

DAILY ACTION SHEETS

ONE LAUNCH METHOD

DATE TODAY: ————————————————

MOVE YOUR BUSINESS FORWARD:

APPOINTMENTS:

☐ _____

☐ _____

☐ _____

☐ _____

☐ _____

☐ _____

☐ _____

☐ _____

NEW CONTACTS AND FOLLOW UP:

DAILY ACTION SHEETS

ONE LAUNCH METHOD

DATE TODAY: _____

MOVE YOUR BUSINESS FORWARD:

APPOINTMENTS:

- [ ] _____
- [ ] _____
- [ ] _____
- [ ] _____
- [ ] _____
- [ ] _____
- [ ] _____
- [ ] _____

NEW CONTACTS AND FOLLOW UP:

DAILY ACTION SHEETS

ONE LAUNCH METHOD

DATE TODAY: ———————————

MOVE YOUR BUSINESS FORWARD:

APPOINTMENTS:

- [ ] _____
- [ ] _____
- [ ] _____
- [ ] _____
- [ ] _____
- [ ] _____
- [ ] _____
- [ ] _____

NEW CONTACTS AND FOLLOW UP:

DAILY ACTION SHEETS

ONE LAUNCH METHOD

DATE TODAY: ─────────────

MOVE YOUR BUSINESS FORWARD: APPOINTMENTS:

☐ _____

☐ _____

☐ _____

☐ _____

☐ _____

☐ _____

☐ _____

☐ _____

NEW CONTACTS AND FOLLOW UP:

DAILY ACTION SHEETS

ONE LAUNCH METHOD

DATE TODAY: _____

MOVE YOUR BUSINESS FORWARD:

- [ ] _____
- [ ] _____
- [ ] _____
- [ ] _____
- [ ] _____
- [ ] _____
- [ ] _____
- [ ] _____

APPOINTMENTS:

NEW CONTACTS AND FOLLOW UP:

DAILY ACTION SHEETS

ONE LAUNCH METHOD

DATE TODAY: ────────────────

MOVE YOUR BUSINESS FORWARD:

- [ ] _____
- [ ] _____
- [ ] _____
- [ ] _____
- [ ] _____
- [ ] _____
- [ ] _____
- [ ] _____

APPOINTMENTS:

NEW CONTACTS AND FOLLOW UP:

DAILY ACTION SHEETS

ONE LAUNCH METHOD

DATE TODAY: ―――――――――

MOVE YOUR BUSINESS FORWARD:

APPOINTMENTS:

- [ ] _____
- [ ] _____
- [ ] _____
- [ ] _____
- [ ] _____
- [ ] _____
- [ ] _____
- [ ] _____

NEW CONTACTS AND FOLLOW UP:

DAILY ACTION SHEETS

ONE LAUNCH METHOD

DATE TODAY: ———————————

MOVE YOUR BUSINESS FORWARD: APPOINTMENTS:

- [ ] _____
- [ ] _____
- [ ] _____
- [ ] _____
- [ ] _____
- [ ] _____
- [ ] _____
- [ ] _____

NEW CONTACTS AND FOLLOW UP:

DAILY ACTION SHEETS

ONE LAUNCH METHOD

DATE TODAY: ───────────────

MOVE YOUR BUSINESS FORWARD:

APPOINTMENTS:

- [ ] _____
- [ ] _____
- [ ] _____
- [ ] _____
- [ ] _____
- [ ] _____
- [ ] _____
- [ ] _____

NEW CONTACTS AND FOLLOW UP:

DAILY ACTION SHEETS

ONE LAUNCH METHOD

DATE TODAY: ―――――――――

MOVE YOUR BUSINESS FORWARD:

APPOINTMENTS:

☐ _____

☐ _____

☐ _____

☐ _____

☐ _____

☐ _____

☐ _____

☐ _____

NEW CONTACTS AND FOLLOW UP:

DAILY ACTION SHEETS

ONE LAUNCH METHOD

DATE TODAY: _____

MOVE YOUR BUSINESS FORWARD:

- [ ] _____
- [ ] _____
- [ ] _____
- [ ] _____
- [ ] _____
- [ ] _____
- [ ] _____
- [ ] _____

APPOINTMENTS:

NEW CONTACTS AND FOLLOW UP:

DAILY ACTION SHEETS

ONE LAUNCH METHOD

DATE TODAY: ─────────────

MOVE YOUR BUSINESS FORWARD:

APPOINTMENTS:

- [ ] _____
- [ ] _____
- [ ] _____
- [ ] _____
- [ ] _____
- [ ] _____
- [ ] _____
- [ ] _____

NEW CONTACTS AND FOLLOW UP:

DAILY ACTION SHEETS

ONE LAUNCH METHOD

DATE TODAY: ───────────

MOVE YOUR BUSINESS FORWARD:

- [ ] _____
- [ ] _____
- [ ] _____
- [ ] _____
- [ ] _____
- [ ] _____
- [ ] _____
- [ ] _____

APPOINTMENTS:

NEW CONTACTS AND FOLLOW UP:

DAILY ACTION SHEETS

ONE LAUNCH METHOD

DATE TODAY: ————————————

MOVE YOUR BUSINESS FORWARD: APPOINTMENTS:

☐ _____

☐ _____

☐ _____

☐ _____

☐ _____

☐ _____

☐ _____

☐ _____

NEW CONTACTS AND FOLLOW UP:

DAILY ACTION SHEETS

ONE LAUNCH METHOD

DATE TODAY: ─────────────

MOVE YOUR BUSINESS FORWARD:

☐ _____

☐ _____

☐ _____

☐ _____

☐ _____

☐ _____

☐ _____

☐ _____

APPOINTMENTS:

NEW CONTACTS AND FOLLOW UP:

DAILY ACTION SHEETS

ONE LAUNCH METHOD

DATE TODAY: ━━━━━━━━━━

MOVE YOUR BUSINESS FORWARD:

APPOINTMENTS:

- [ ] _____
- [ ] _____
- [ ] _____
- [ ] _____
- [ ] _____
- [ ] _____
- [ ] _____
- [ ] _____

NEW CONTACTS AND FOLLOW UP:

DAILY ACTION SHEETS

ONE LAUNCH METHOD

DATE TODAY: _____

MOVE YOUR BUSINESS FORWARD:

- [ ] _____
- [ ] _____
- [ ] _____
- [ ] _____
- [ ] _____
- [ ] _____
- [ ] _____
- [ ] _____

APPOINTMENTS:

NEW CONTACTS AND FOLLOW UP:

DAILY ACTION SHEETS

ONE LAUNCH METHOD

DATE TODAY: ⎯⎯⎯⎯⎯⎯⎯⎯⎯

MOVE YOUR BUSINESS FORWARD:

☐ _____

☐ _____

☐ _____

☐ _____

☐ _____

☐ _____

☐ _____

☐ _____

APPOINTMENTS:

NEW CONTACTS AND FOLLOW UP:

DAILY ACTION SHEETS

ONE LAUNCH METHOD

DATE TODAY: _____

MOVE YOUR BUSINESS FORWARD:

- [ ] _____
- [ ] _____
- [ ] _____
- [ ] _____
- [ ] _____
- [ ] _____
- [ ] _____
- [ ] _____

APPOINTMENTS:

NEW CONTACTS AND FOLLOW UP:

DAILY ACTION SHEETS

ONE LAUNCH METHOD

DATE TODAY: ─────────────

MOVE YOUR BUSINESS FORWARD:

APPOINTMENTS:

- [ ] _____
- [ ] _____
- [ ] _____
- [ ] _____
- [ ] _____
- [ ] _____
- [ ] _____
- [ ] _____

NEW CONTACTS AND FOLLOW UP:

DAILY ACTION SHEETS

ONE LAUNCH METHOD

DATE TODAY: ─────────────

MOVE YOUR BUSINESS FORWARD:

- ☐ _____
- ☐ _____
- ☐ _____
- ☐ _____
- ☐ _____
- ☐ _____
- ☐ _____
- ☐ _____

APPOINTMENTS:

NEW CONTACTS AND FOLLOW UP:

DAILY ACTION SHEETS

ONE LAUNCH METHOD

DATE TODAY: ———————————

MOVE YOUR BUSINESS FORWARD:

- ☐ _____
- ☐ _____
- ☐ _____
- ☐ _____
- ☐ _____
- ☐ _____
- ☐ _____
- ☐ _____

APPOINTMENTS:

NEW CONTACTS AND FOLLOW UP:

DAILY ACTION SHEETS

ONE LAUNCH METHOD

DATE TODAY: ——————————————

MOVE YOUR BUSINESS FORWARD:

- [ ] _____
- [ ] _____
- [ ] _____
- [ ] _____
- [ ] _____
- [ ] _____
- [ ] _____
- [ ] _____

APPOINTMENTS:

NEW CONTACTS AND FOLLOW UP:

DAILY ACTION SHEETS

ONE LAUNCH METHOD

DATE TODAY: ———————————

MOVE YOUR BUSINESS FORWARD:

APPOINTMENTS:

- ☐ _____
- ☐ _____
- ☐ _____
- ☐ _____
- ☐ _____
- ☐ _____
- ☐ _____
- ☐ _____

NEW CONTACTS AND FOLLOW UP:

DAILY ACTION SHEETS

ONE LAUNCH METHOD

DATE TODAY: _____

MOVE YOUR BUSINESS FORWARD:

- [ ] _____
- [ ] _____
- [ ] _____
- [ ] _____
- [ ] _____
- [ ] _____
- [ ] _____
- [ ] _____

APPOINTMENTS:

NEW CONTACTS AND FOLLOW UP:

DAILY ACTION SHEETS

ONE LAUNCH METHOD

DATE TODAY: ―――――――――

MOVE YOUR BUSINESS FORWARD:

☐ _____

☐ _____

☐ _____

☐ _____

☐ _____

☐ _____

☐ _____

☐ _____

APPOINTMENTS:

NEW CONTACTS AND FOLLOW UP:

DAILY ACTION SHEETS

ONE LAUNCH METHOD

DATE TODAY: ─────────────

MOVE YOUR BUSINESS FORWARD:

APPOINTMENTS:

☐ _____

☐ _____

☐ _____

☐ _____

☐ _____

☐ _____

☐ _____

☐ _____

NEW CONTACTS AND FOLLOW UP:

DAILY ACTION SHEETS

ONE LAUNCH METHOD

DATE TODAY: ━━━━━━━━━

MOVE YOUR BUSINESS FORWARD:

APPOINTMENTS:

- [ ] _____
- [ ] _____
- [ ] _____
- [ ] _____
- [ ] _____
- [ ] _____
- [ ] _____
- [ ] _____

NEW CONTACTS AND FOLLOW UP:

DAILY ACTION SHEETS

ONE LAUNCH METHOD

DATE TODAY: _____

MOVE YOUR BUSINESS FORWARD:

- ☐ _____
- ☐ _____
- ☐ _____
- ☐ _____
- ☐ _____
- ☐ _____
- ☐ _____
- ☐ _____

APPOINTMENTS:

NEW CONTACTS AND FOLLOW UP:

DAILY ACTION SHEETS

ONE LAUNCH METHOD

DATE TODAY: ⎯⎯⎯⎯⎯⎯⎯⎯⎯⎯⎯

MOVE YOUR BUSINESS FORWARD:

APPOINTMENTS:

- [ ] _____
- [ ] _____
- [ ] _____
- [ ] _____
- [ ] _____
- [ ] _____
- [ ] _____
- [ ] _____

NEW CONTACTS AND FOLLOW UP:

DAILY ACTION SHEETS

ONE LAUNCH METHOD

DATE TODAY: _____

MOVE YOUR BUSINESS FORWARD:

APPOINTMENTS:

- [ ] _____
- [ ] _____
- [ ] _____
- [ ] _____
- [ ] _____
- [ ] _____
- [ ] _____
- [ ] _____

NEW CONTACTS AND FOLLOW UP:

DAILY ACTION SHEETS

ONE LAUNCH METHOD

DATE TODAY: ━━━━━━━━━━

MOVE YOUR BUSINESS FORWARD:

- ☐ _____
- ☐ _____
- ☐ _____
- ☐ _____
- ☐ _____
- ☐ _____
- ☐ _____
- ☐ _____

APPOINTMENTS:

NEW CONTACTS AND FOLLOW UP:

DAILY ACTION SHEETS

ONE LAUNCH METHOD

DATE TODAY: _____

MOVE YOUR BUSINESS FORWARD:

APPOINTMENTS:

- ☐ _____
- ☐ _____
- ☐ _____
- ☐ _____
- ☐ _____
- ☐ _____
- ☐ _____
- ☐ _____

NEW CONTACTS AND FOLLOW UP:

DAILY ACTION SHEETS

ONE LAUNCH METHOD

DATE TODAY: _____

MOVE YOUR BUSINESS FORWARD: APPOINTMENTS:

☐ _____

☐ _____

☐ _____

☐ _____

☐ _____

☐ _____

☐ _____

☐ _____

NEW CONTACTS AND FOLLOW UP:

DAILY ACTION SHEETS

ONE LAUNCH METHOD

DATE TODAY: ———————————

MOVE YOUR BUSINESS FORWARD:

APPOINTMENTS:

- [ ] _____
- [ ] _____
- [ ] _____
- [ ] _____
- [ ] _____
- [ ] _____
- [ ] _____
- [ ] _____

NEW CONTACTS AND FOLLOW UP:

DAILY ACTION SHEETS

ONE LAUNCH METHOD

DATE TODAY: —————————————

MOVE YOUR BUSINESS FORWARD:

- [ ] _____
- [ ] _____
- [ ] _____
- [ ] _____
- [ ] _____
- [ ] _____
- [ ] _____
- [ ] _____

APPOINTMENTS:

NEW CONTACTS AND FOLLOW UP:

DAILY ACTION SHEETS

ONE LAUNCH METHOD

DATE TODAY: _____

MOVE YOUR BUSINESS FORWARD:

APPOINTMENTS:

- [ ] _____
- [ ] _____
- [ ] _____
- [ ] _____
- [ ] _____
- [ ] _____
- [ ] _____
- [ ] _____

NEW CONTACTS AND FOLLOW UP:

DAILY ACTION SHEETS

ONE LAUNCH METHOD

DATE TODAY: ────────────

MOVE YOUR BUSINESS FORWARD:

APPOINTMENTS:

☐ _____

☐ _____

☐ _____

☐ _____

☐ _____

☐ _____

☐ _____

☐ _____

NEW CONTACTS AND FOLLOW UP:

DAILY ACTION SHEETS

ONE LAUNCH METHOD

DATE TODAY: _____

MOVE YOUR BUSINESS FORWARD:

- [ ] _____
- [ ] _____
- [ ] _____
- [ ] _____
- [ ] _____
- [ ] _____
- [ ] _____
- [ ] _____

APPOINTMENTS:

NEW CONTACTS AND FOLLOW UP:

DAILY ACTION SHEETS

ONE LAUNCH METHOD

DATE TODAY: ⸻

MOVE YOUR BUSINESS FORWARD:

APPOINTMENTS:

- [ ] _____
- [ ] _____
- [ ] _____
- [ ] _____
- [ ] _____
- [ ] _____
- [ ] _____
- [ ] _____

NEW CONTACTS AND FOLLOW UP:

DAILY ACTION SHEETS

ONE LAUNCH METHOD

DATE TODAY: _____

MOVE YOUR BUSINESS FORWARD: APPOINTMENTS:

☐ _____

☐ _____

☐ _____

☐ _____

☐ _____

☐ _____

☐ _____

☐ _____

NEW CONTACTS AND FOLLOW UP:

DAILY ACTION SHEETS

ONE LAUNCH METHOD

DATE TODAY: ───────────────

MOVE YOUR BUSINESS FORWARD:

APPOINTMENTS:

- [ ] _____
- [ ] _____
- [ ] _____
- [ ] _____
- [ ] _____
- [ ] _____
- [ ] _____
- [ ] _____

NEW CONTACTS AND FOLLOW UP:

DAILY ACTION SHEETS

ONE LAUNCH METHOD

DATE TODAY: ————————————

MOVE YOUR BUSINESS FORWARD: APPOINTMENTS:

- ☐ _____
- ☐ _____
- ☐ _____
- ☐ _____
- ☐ _____
- ☐ _____
- ☐ _____
- ☐ _____

NEW CONTACTS AND FOLLOW UP:

DAILY ACTION SHEETS

ONE LAUNCH METHOD

DATE TODAY: ————————————

MOVE YOUR BUSINESS FORWARD:

- [ ] _____
- [ ] _____
- [ ] _____
- [ ] _____
- [ ] _____
- [ ] _____
- [ ] _____
- [ ] _____

APPOINTMENTS:

NEW CONTACTS AND FOLLOW UP:

DAILY ACTION SHEETS

ONE LAUNCH METHOD

DATE TODAY: _____

MOVE YOUR BUSINESS FORWARD: APPOINTMENTS:

☐ _____

☐ _____

☐ _____

☐ _____

☐ _____

☐ _____

☐ _____

☐ _____

NEW CONTACTS AND FOLLOW UP:

DAILY ACTION SHEETS

ONE LAUNCH METHOD

DATE TODAY: ───────────

MOVE YOUR BUSINESS FORWARD:

☐ _____

☐ _____

☐ _____

☐ _____

☐ _____

☐ _____

☐ _____

☐ _____

APPOINTMENTS:

NEW CONTACTS AND FOLLOW UP:

DAILY ACTION SHEETS

ONE LAUNCH METHOD

DATE TODAY: ————————

MOVE YOUR BUSINESS FORWARD:

☐ _____

☐ _____

☐ _____

☐ _____

☐ _____

☐ _____

☐ _____

☐ _____

APPOINTMENTS:

NEW CONTACTS AND FOLLOW UP:

DAILY ACTION SHEETS

ONE LAUNCH METHOD

DATE TODAY: ————————

MOVE YOUR BUSINESS FORWARD:

- [ ] _____
- [ ] _____
- [ ] _____
- [ ] _____
- [ ] _____
- [ ] _____
- [ ] _____
- [ ] _____

APPOINTMENTS:

NEW CONTACTS AND FOLLOW UP:

DAILY ACTION SHEETS

ONE LAUNCH METHOD

DATE TODAY: ─────────────

MOVE YOUR BUSINESS FORWARD:

APPOINTMENTS:

- ☐ _____
- ☐ _____
- ☐ _____
- ☐ _____
- ☐ _____
- ☐ _____
- ☐ _____
- ☐ _____

NEW CONTACTS AND FOLLOW UP:

DAILY ACTION SHEETS

ONE LAUNCH METHOD

DATE TODAY: ———————

MOVE YOUR BUSINESS FORWARD:

APPOINTMENTS:

☐ _____

☐ _____

☐ _____

☐ _____

☐ _____

☐ _____

☐ _____

☐ _____

NEW CONTACTS AND FOLLOW UP:

DAILY ACTION SHEETS

ONE LAUNCH METHOD

DATE TODAY: ─────────────

MOVE YOUR BUSINESS FORWARD:

- ☐ _____
- ☐ _____
- ☐ _____
- ☐ _____
- ☐ _____
- ☐ _____
- ☐ _____
- ☐ _____

APPOINTMENTS:

NEW CONTACTS AND FOLLOW UP:

DAILY ACTION SHEETS

ONE LAUNCH METHOD

DATE TODAY: _____

MOVE YOUR BUSINESS FORWARD:

☐ _____

☐ _____

☐ _____

☐ _____

☐ _____

☐ _____

☐ _____

☐ _____

APPOINTMENTS:

NEW CONTACTS AND FOLLOW UP:

DAILY ACTION SHEETS

ONE LAUNCH METHOD

DATE TODAY: _____

MOVE YOUR BUSINESS FORWARD:

APPOINTMENTS:

- [ ] _____
- [ ] _____
- [ ] _____
- [ ] _____
- [ ] _____
- [ ] _____
- [ ] _____
- [ ] _____

NEW CONTACTS AND FOLLOW UP:

DAILY ACTION SHEETS

ONE LAUNCH METHOD

DATE TODAY: ───────────

MOVE YOUR BUSINESS FORWARD: APPOINTMENTS:

☐ _____

☐ _____

☐ _____

☐ _____

☐ _____

☐ _____

☐ _____

☐ _____

NEW CONTACTS AND FOLLOW UP:

DAILY ACTION SHEETS

ONE LAUNCH METHOD

DATE TODAY: _____

MOVE YOUR BUSINESS FORWARD:

APPOINTMENTS:

- [ ] _____
- [ ] _____
- [ ] _____
- [ ] _____
- [ ] _____
- [ ] _____
- [ ] _____
- [ ] _____

NEW CONTACTS AND FOLLOW UP:

DAILY ACTION SHEETS

ONE LAUNCH METHOD

DATE TODAY: _____

MOVE YOUR BUSINESS FORWARD:

- [ ] _____
- [ ] _____
- [ ] _____
- [ ] _____
- [ ] _____
- [ ] _____
- [ ] _____
- [ ] _____

APPOINTMENTS:

NEW CONTACTS AND FOLLOW UP:

DAILY ACTION SHEETS

ONE LAUNCH METHOD

DATE TODAY: _____

MOVE YOUR BUSINESS FORWARD:

APPOINTMENTS:

- [ ] _____
- [ ] _____
- [ ] _____
- [ ] _____
- [ ] _____
- [ ] _____
- [ ] _____
- [ ] _____

NEW CONTACTS AND FOLLOW UP:

DAILY ACTION SHEETS

ONE LAUNCH METHOD

DATE TODAY: ⎯⎯⎯⎯⎯⎯⎯⎯⎯

MOVE YOUR BUSINESS FORWARD:

APPOINTMENTS:

☐ _____

☐ _____

☐ _____

☐ _____

☐ _____

☐ _____

☐ _____

☐ _____

NEW CONTACTS AND FOLLOW UP:

DAILY ACTION SHEETS

ONE LAUNCH METHOD

DATE TODAY: ───────────────

MOVE YOUR BUSINESS FORWARD:

APPOINTMENTS:

- [ ] _____
- [ ] _____
- [ ] _____
- [ ] _____
- [ ] _____
- [ ] _____
- [ ] _____
- [ ] _____

NEW CONTACTS AND FOLLOW UP:

DAILY ACTION SHEETS

ONE LAUNCH METHOD

DATE TODAY: ─────────────

MOVE YOUR BUSINESS FORWARD:

APPOINTMENTS:

- [ ] _____
- [ ] _____
- [ ] _____
- [ ] _____
- [ ] _____
- [ ] _____
- [ ] _____
- [ ] _____

NEW CONTACTS AND FOLLOW UP:

DAILY ACTION SHEETS

ONE LAUNCH METHOD

DATE TODAY: ─────────────

MOVE YOUR BUSINESS FORWARD:

APPOINTMENTS:

☐ _____

☐ _____

☐ _____

☐ _____

☐ _____

☐ _____

☐ _____

☐ _____

NEW CONTACTS AND FOLLOW UP:

DAILY ACTION SHEETS

ONE LAUNCH METHOD

DATE TODAY: ——————————

MOVE YOUR BUSINESS FORWARD:

☐ _____

☐ _____

☐ _____

☐ _____

☐ _____

☐ _____

☐ _____

☐ _____

APPOINTMENTS:

NEW CONTACTS AND FOLLOW UP:

DAILY ACTION SHEETS

ONE LAUNCH METHOD

DATE TODAY: _____

MOVE YOUR BUSINESS FORWARD:

- [ ] _____
- [ ] _____
- [ ] _____
- [ ] _____
- [ ] _____
- [ ] _____
- [ ] _____
- [ ] _____

APPOINTMENTS:

NEW CONTACTS AND FOLLOW UP:

DAILY ACTION SHEETS

ONE LAUNCH METHOD

DATE TODAY: —————————————

MOVE YOUR BUSINESS FORWARD: APPOINTMENTS:

☐ _____

☐ _____

☐ _____

☐ _____

☐ _____

☐ _____

☐ _____

☐ _____

NEW CONTACTS AND FOLLOW UP:

DAILY ACTION SHEETS

ONE LAUNCH METHOD

DATE TODAY: ————————————

MOVE YOUR BUSINESS FORWARD:

☐ _____

☐ _____

☐ _____

☐ _____

☐ _____

☐ _____

☐ _____

☐ _____

APPOINTMENTS:

NEW CONTACTS AND FOLLOW UP:

About the Author

Leslie Klatt is the go-to Business Launch Strategist that coaches, service providers and online business owners have been waiting for, if you haven't already worked with her for your product, service, or online business success. With a proven track record, Leslie is amongst the Top 1% of Business Strategists in North America.

The One Launch Method stems from her solid background in corporate business, where organisations play for longevity and sustainability, building brand credibility and a high profile as the 'go to' market and project management leaders.

WORK WITH ME

One Launch Method with Leslie Klatt

One Launch
Done for you

Three month service
Let my team do the work for you.
Weekly coaching and guidance for set up and delivery.
One year of support.

One Launch
Done with you

Three month service
You or your team will follow through with the plan.
Weekly coaching and guidance for set up and delivery.
One year of support.

One Launch VIP

Twelve month service
Membership of exclusive online community.
Weekly Group coaching calls
One year of support.

FOLLOW ME
Online

www.leslieklatt.com

fb.com/leslieklattceo

ig.com/leslieklattlife

Made in the USA
Monee, IL
26 May 2021